THE SIMPLE GUIDE TO
IRELAND
CUSTOMS AND ETIQUETTE

COVER ILLUSTRATION

Traditional Irish dancing and folk music have been enjoying a renaissance since 'Riverdance' (p. 13)

ABOUT THE AUTHOR

AIDAN McNAMARA is an Irish writer with roots in Cork and Tipperary. A keen observer of Irish life for many years, he has extensive experience in the private and public sectors, both in Ireland and abroad.

ILLUSTRATED BY
PETER SEARLE

SIMPLE GUIDE TO

IRELAND

CUSTOMS & ETIQUETTE

AIDAN McNAMARA

GLOBAL BOOKS LTD

Simple Guides • Series 1
CUSTOMS & ETIQUETTE

The Simple Guide to
IRELAND
CUSTOMS & ETIQUETTE
by Aidan McNamara

First edition 1996

Second Edition 2000 by
GLOBAL BOOKS LTD
PO Box 219, Folkestone, Kent, England CT20 3LZ

ISBN 1–86034–066–0

British Library Cataloguing in Publication Data
A CIP catalogue entry for this book
is available from the British Library

Set in Futura 11 on 12 pt by Bookman, Hayes, Middlesex
Printed in Malta by Interprint Ltd

Contents

Preface

Thomas MacDonough

by

FRANCIS LEDWIDGE

He shall not hear the bittern cry
In the wild sky, where he is lain,
Nor voices of the sweeter birds
Above the wailing of the rain.

Nor shall he know when wild March blows
Thro' slanting snows her fanfare shrill,
Blowing to flame the golden cup
Of many an upset daffodil.

But when the dark cow leaves the moor,
And pastures poor with greedy weeds,
Perhaps he'll hear her low at morn
Lifting her head in pleasant meads.

I have chosen this poem to go at the front of this book because it represents so many aspects of Ireland.

It is short and lyrical and, despite lengthy Irish masterpieces such as James Joyce's *Ulysses* or Bram Stoker's *Dracula*, much Irish inspiration is essentially short and lyrical. Technically, it displays the beauty of internal rhyme (the rhyming of the last word of a line with a word in the middle of the next line), carried over into English from Irish (Gaelic) poetry.

Medieval Irish monks, bored with the slow, painstaking skills they had to exercise in copying out elaborate versions of the Gospels, created the earliest vernacular literature in Western Europe by scribbling short lyrics in the margins of their work. At the same time, they also displayed remarkable artistic talents in the way they illustrated, or 'illuminated', the Gospel transcriptions. The *Book of Kells* (see p.94) is considered the most outstanding example of this particular artform.

The Francis Ledwidge poem is about death and the Irish, it has to be said, for all the liveliness of their appetite for life, do have a deeply melancholic streak. Death, with its elaborate funerals and public grief, has a central place in Irish life.

It is a lament for a man, Thomas MacDonagh, himself a young poet, shot by the British in 1916 for his part in the abortive rising against their rule: He is one of the inspirational martyrs of Irish nationalism, the force of which still reverberates on the island today.

Strangely enough, it was written by a man who lost his own life the following year, fighting in the British Army during the First World War, as did hundreds of his fellow Irishmen, illustrating the complexity of Irish history, a complexity recognized in the Good Friday Agreement of 1998, which aims to exorcise the demons of Irish history and provide a means by which all people on the island can live together in peace and prosperity.

I have placed Ledwidge's poem at the beginning of this book because it is beautiful and because it is optimistic; indeed, optimism has never been more evident in Irish life than it is these days. The fact also that it was one of my father's favourite poems and has echoed in my own head for years is neither here nor there.

☐

In this second, enlarged edition, I have had the opportunity both to update the text throughout where necessary, as well as expand on certain topics because of the additional space available. For example, I have been able to give a fuller account of the history of Ireland (Ch.2), I have added a new section to Society (Ch.3) on the 'Irish View of the Outside World', as well as a new section to Personal Relationships (Ch.4) on 'Home Life and Attitude to Children'. I was also glad of the opportunity to highlight some of Ireland's famous landmarks and treasures (Ch.11) under the heading 'The Wonders of Ireland'. Nobody will blame me for that! There is also a collection of traditional Irish songs (lyrics only) for general interest and amusement on pages 89-93.

A.M.
Spring 2000

1

Introduction: Today's Ireland

Sandwiched between Britain and America, the pattern of life in Ireland is similar in most important respects to its neighbours: of similar racial stock, we speak the same language, and we dress and consume in almost identical fashion most of the time.

This has become particularly evident in the last forty years, during which time Ireland has moved from a highly protectionist state economically, with a predictably insular psychology, to a position where merchandise exports represent

Map of Ireland

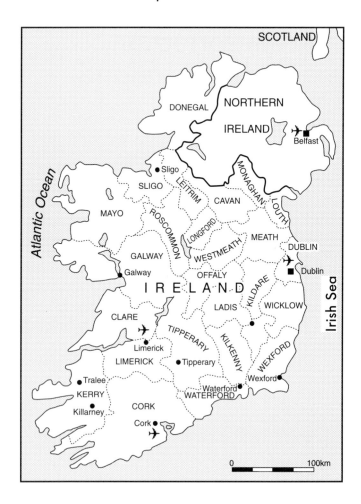

nearly 70% of GNP, while the population is ever more highly educated and adaptable, with a thirst for the good things of life – not least foreign travel.

To anyone who knew the country in the 1950s, the transformation could well appear little short of miraculous. Yet it continues at breakneck speed.

Religion remains an important factor in Irish life generally but the traditional pervasive influence of the Roman Catholic Church in southern Irish life is rapidly loosening and a liberal, pluralistic, ethic is gaining dominance and church-going declines among the younger generation.

Television has been a driving force behind social change. Irish television has played a role, especially the 'Late Late Show', which provided a forum for debating the essential issues of Irish life for more than a generation.

Probably of greater significance, however, has been the widespread availability of British television through cable in the urban areas, especially Dublin, with a high proportion of these households cabled for over twenty years. There is no doubt, therefore, that television has helped form the consciousness of the younger generation – now a majority of the population – and profoundly influences the evolution of society.

Membership of the European Union has been another factor of enormous importance in the transformation of Ireland. The EU has certainly benefited the country economically, as the rapidly improving road network bears witness. The EU has also imposed standards in areas such as sexual equality. But its impact runs much deeper. It has enabled Ireland to diversify away from a some-what claustrophobic one-to-one relationship with Britain and to emerge as a modern *European* country, increasingly confident of her own distinctive identity.

At the time of writing, the Irish economy is continuing to perform exceptionally well and seems likely to continue doing so for the foreseeable future. Tourism, in particular, is enjoying a wonderful boom period throughout the island, which is marketed as a single entity by the tourist industry worldwide.

Hot Tip: Experience Ireland's 'Buzz'!

Most visitors to Ireland experience a buzz, an invigorating electricity in the air. It is undeniable. This was evident to hundreds of millions of viewers around the globe who watched Ireland's hosting of the Eurovision Song Contest, following its record-breaking run of successes in the early 1990s.

Irish music, often fusing the traditional with modern forms, including rock-n-roll, has created world-class performers such as Van Morrison, U2, Sinead O'Connor, the Corrs and the Cranberries. In literature, writers like Roddy Doyle are managing to combine popular appeal with serious analysis of contemporary urban society. *Riverdance*, which began life as the Interval entertainment of the Eurovision Song Contest in 1994 and went on to take London by storm as a full-length concert in 1995–6, has worked the same magic, fusing the traditional and innovative to create a new artform in Irish dance.

'Riverdance'

This, then, is the Ireland that the visitor will encounter. Confident of its destiny as a modern European country, a society which values tradition but understands also the need to grasp change and exploit the power of innovation.

Hot Tip: The Reward is in the Detail

Ireland is also a complex place, where the apparent similarity to other developed Western countries can sometimes be misleading. It is a place where a little trouble taken to learn its customs, etiquette and traditions could be amply rewarded.

Having said that, the best thing that a visitor can do in Ireland is to relax and be themselves. A foreigner cannot become Irish by a process of osmosis and is certainly not expected to master all the subtleties of the local culture. As in many other cultures, the foreigner in Ireland is granted a sort of general dispensation to be different, of which they should take full advantage. Do not worry too much, therefore, about protocol: go out and enjoy yourself; that is exactly what the Irish themselves are trying to do!

Most of the content of this guide refers to the Republic of Ireland only. As part, *de facto*, of the United Kingdom, Northern Ireland has so many differences that it would require a separate volume to do justice to it.

2

A Bit of History

Megalithic tomb, Newgrange

Ireland is believed to have been inhabited since about 7,000 BC. The Neolithic or Stone-Age inhabitants, who constructed massive religious monuments such as the megalithic tomb at Newgrange (within easy driving distance of Dublin and well worth a visit), came around 4,000 years later. The Celts arrived about the sixth century BC and ushered in a dynamic era of early civilization. Ireland has, for example, the largest collection of prehistoric gold artifacts found in Western and Northern Europe; visitors who can spare the time are strongly recommended to see them at the National Museum in central Dublin.

With the introduction of Christianity in the fifth century came literacy and the classical learning of Greco-Roman civilization which fused with the Celtic tradition to produce such masterpieces as the *Book of Kells* which can be seen at Trinity College, Dublin, and the Ardagh Chalice.

Ardagh Chalice

From the following century, Irish missionaries played a prominent role in the Christianization of the rest of Europe. At home, this was the fabled era of 'saints and scholars'.

The Viking intrusions from the ninth century brought death and destruction but also trade, currency and the foundation of most of the country's major towns.

The Norman invasion of the late twelfth century resulted in much of Ireland coming under English rule but it was not until the Tudor era of the sixteenth century that Ireland was brought fully under control.

Hot Tip: The Key to Understanding Ireland's Divisions

From the Reformation (1642–58) to the French Revolution (1789), the Anglican English state regarded Roman Catholicism as a major threat of subversion. The majority in Ireland, who remained stubbornly Roman Catholic, were victimized by the Penal Laws against religions other than Anglicism and a series of 'Plantations' were implemented which aimed at replacing them with loyal Protestants. The problem of division among people on the island of Ireland, still tragically evident in Northern Ireland, dates from this era.

The influence of the American and French Revolutions impacted on Ireland in the late eighteenth century when the United Irishmen attempted to unite the two traditions in an independent Ireland. The failed rebellion of 1798 led instead to Ireland being incorporated into the United Kingdom of Ireland and Britain under the Act of Union (1801).

Daniel O'Connell achieved basic civil rights for the majority of the population with Catholic Emancipation (1829) but failed in his efforts to use parliamentary means to achieve the repeal of the Act of Union.

This failure, together with the devastating famine of 1845-9 which killed one million people and led a further million to emigrate, undermined popular faith in politics as a means of achieving constitutional change. Nevertheless, the Irish Parliamentary Party, under Charles Stewart Parnell, had overwhelming popular support among the nationalist majority of the population for achieving Home Rule (autonomy in many areas within the United Kingdom framework).

Unionist opposition, largely concentrated in the north-eastern part of the island, and the outbreak of the First World War led to the Home Rule legislation being shelved. The execution of the leaders of the 1916 Rising in Dublin was part of a chain of events which irrevocably alienated Irish public opinion from British rule.

A guerrilla war, conducted under the legendary leadership of Michael Collins, together with the strength of American public opinion, now a powerful force in Anglo-Irish relations, led to twenty-six of the thirty-two counties in Ireland being granted independent statehood in 1921. The other six, with a Unionist majority, remained in union with Britain.

FROM VALERA TO THE EU

The dominant figure in Irish politics in the decades after independence was Eamon De Valera, whose 1937 constitution expanded the freedom gained in 1921 and profoundly influenced the subsequent development of the Irish state. In the economic sphere, his protectionist policies were seen to be inadequate for further development by the late 1950s and, in the early 1960s, Ireland embraced free trade and set about attracting foreign investment.

Together with membership of the European Union (from 1973) and consistent investment in education since the late 1960s, these decisions laid the foundations for Ireland's remarkable development, in the last decade of the twentieth century especially, which has seen it jump from one of the poorest to one of richest EU member states in the span of a generation.

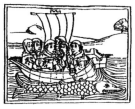

Sixth-century Irish saint, St Brendan, on one of his many voyages.
[Woodcut of 1476]

Hot Tip: Ireland's Populations

The population of the Republic of Ireland today is just under four million, the majority of whom are Roman Catholic. The population of Northern Ireland consists of around 1.5 million, with a majority of Protestants who generally desire union with Britain, and a significant Roman Catholic minority (over 40%), mostly nationalist, desiring union with the Republic.

Political instability in Northern Ireland has given rise to violence sporadically since 1921. The longest period of violence lasted from the late 1960s to 1994, when the Republican (IRA) and Unionist paramilitaries declared open-ended ceasefires. This has given rise to optimism that the long-term political settlement, covering the internal situation in Northern Ireland, relations between Northern Ireland and the Republic, and between Britain and Ireland, can come to fruition.

The harp – emblem of Ireland

The Good Friday Agreement of 1998 provided a three-stranded solution, consisting of an elected Assembly and Executive, representative of both political traditions in Northern Ireland; cross-border bodies to develop cooperation between both parts of the island; and an East-West dimension designed to improve relationships between the islands of Ireland and Britain. The Agreement became operational in late 1999, but was suspended after a little over two months because of decommissioning problems.

3

Society

Georgian house in Dublin

The Anglo-Irish élite, which once gave Ireland an aristocracy much like its English counterpart, has now largely died out. At the same time, the Victorian industrialization, which created the distinctive working-class/middle-class division in English society, largely by-passed Ireland, except, to some extent, in what is now Northern Ireland.

The result is that Irish society today is fairly heterogeneous, with most people within the last few generations having roughly similar roots in rural culture.

Status is derived primarily either from wealth or talent; by and large, what you can achieve will be determined by what you are rather than by your background or education.

Heredity is important, especially in politics and the professions such as law and medicine. By and large, however, those perceived to be at the top of Irish society come from the new class of entrepreneurs, some of whom are extremely wealthy by any international yardstick. Running in parallel with these developments have been some imaginative retrospective reinvention of genealogies (the poet, W.B. Yeats, provides a good example of middle-class thirst for aristocratic roots) but it is a limited phenomenon.

W.B. Yeats 1900 (after a portrait by John Butler Yeats)

Dublin in the new millennium is awash with new money as successful entrepreneurs and entertainers pay lavish sums for the houses of the old élite in the top residential areas of the city. A traditional Irish irreverent populism continues to act as a great leveller. A conspicuous indifference to star status has drawn to Ireland an increasing number of international celebrities, anxious to move around freely without being mobbed. Film celebrities are also becoming commonplace, as legislation encouraged the development of the film industry.

Hot Tip: Tax Free Art!

Artists, especially writers, are attracted by a provision in the taxation system which allows the income from artistic activity to be tax-free. The presence of so many artists from around the world has been a major cosmopolitan influence on society over the last quarter-century.

The professions probably represent the most traditional element in Irish life, at least as conservative as their counterparts elsewhere. Then there are the so-called 'chattering classes', made up of intellectuals, politicians, bureaucrats, professionals and so forth.

This is an introverted, gossipy world which frequents certain south-side Dublin pubs as well as the 'summer schools'. (A particular Irish institution, the summer schools are devoted mainly to literary pursuits, usually justified in taking place in a given location by dint of its connection with a dead luminary in that field.)

Given Dublin's size a rural/urban divide is inevitable. Country-dwellers often feel misunderstood and maligned by the Dublin-based élite, although this is a declining phenomenon as prosperity percolates through to all parts of the country. As a matter of fact, the epicentre of their distrust is 'Dublin 4', a term which actually refers to a postal area but is meant to sum up the cosmopolitan prejudices (as opposed to sturdy rural values) of the urban élite who live there.

'. . .the new class of entrepreneurs'

But to say that there is no distinctive Irish working-class culture is an exaggeration — the plays of Sean O'Casey and, in our own time, the novels of Roddy Doyle eloquently document the contrary. However, because the dominant ethos was until recently rural, the country has not developed the elaborate rituals of, say, North of England working-class life.

In the countryside, social life is being reinvigorated by a number of factors, including tourism. Now, about one-seventh of the labour force is involved in farming – much higher than the European Union average but a long way removed from the traditional view of Ireland as a predominantly rural society.

THE IRISH VIEW OF THE OUTSIDE WORLD

Parallel with Ireland's huge economic changes had been a remarkable change in the Irish view of the outside world. The decades after independence were marked by a sense of introversion and a desire to concentrate on domestic matters. However, the abandonment of protectionism in the 1960s was also the beginning of a new way of comprehending the outside world.

The young people in Ireland now see the world as their oyster and it is not uncommon for new graduates to spend some years abroad before returning to take up jobs in Ireland. It is perhaps natural that the young Irish should see New York or Sydney as happy hunting grounds but there are substantial pockets of Irish in places as diverse as continental Europe and Japan.

The enthusiastic embrace of the outside world is evident in the music of the Chieftains, which enlists talents from outstanding musical traditions around the world to enliven their performances of Irish traditional music.

The Irish have learned that, not alone do they have nothing to fear from the outside world, but that they and their culture can be enriched by positively embracing it. The world is now a stage on which the Irish can find a global audience for their cultural renaissance and they are enjoying the experience.

Irish prosperity also means that the Irish have to cope with large numbers of foreigners in their midst for the first time; dealing with significant immigration is proving a challenge for a country where emigration was the fate of so many for so long.

$$\boxed{4}$$

Personal Relationships

'Magic. . .take it where you find it'

There *is* magic in Ireland, in the people and the culture, but it is better to take it where you find it rather than to expect it at every turn. Reality, most of the time, is as ordinary in Ireland as anywhere. A burgeoning 'Celtic Tiger' economy dictates that it could not be otherwise.

Bear in mind that young Irish people are, statistically speaking, as likely to have a third-level education as most of their counterparts in the English-speaking world, so there is no more chance of them spending their time dreaming of crocks of gold at the ends of rainbows than anybody else. They have access to the same range of goods and services, eat the same fast food and watch the same movies and TV programmes to be found everywhere. These days they are more likely to be found working in the high-tech sector than on a farm.

Hot Tip: Get the Timing Right!

Irish social events tend to run later than in America or Britain. Guests at a dinner party, for example, should arrive 20–30 minutes after the appointed hour: they will not be expected precisely on time. On the other hand, leaving well before midnight could be interpreted by your hosts as a sign that their party has been deemed by you to have been a failure.

On the subject of timing, an arrangement to meet at a pub at a particular time can be interpreted flexibly: a delay of anything up to an hour would not be considered discourteous.

Given the high cost of alcoholic drink in Ireland, a bottle of wine or spirits makes a particularly welcome gift. If you are going to be in a position to give a gift in Ireland, you could do worse than to avail yourself of your tax-free allowance (if you have any) on the way in!

Greeting in Ireland is generally by handshake although the continental European habit of kissing ladies on the cheek has made inroads in middle- and upper-class circles. The Irish tend to be stiffer about personal contact than, say, the Latin races, but a foreigner, especially if not an Anglo-Saxon, is generally expected to be a bit more flamboyant in these matters!

Personal relations in Ireland are fairly informal: they are more in line with American or Australian norms than some other European countries. People like to get on first-name terms from the beginning. Friendships are formed quickly.

Informality is also the general rule in Irish homes, together with a form of expansiveness which might well see you invited to meet friends, perhaps to play a round of golf or a game of tennis.

Foreigners will find themselves the object of curiosity and will be quickly drawn into conversation – providing they do not wish to stand on ceremony. Rapid-fire conversation, spiced with humour and imagination, is not unusual.

At a deeper level, however, relationships in Ireland, as elsewhere, are governed by class and other considerations. It is also worth making the point that the cheery Hollywood stereotypes, uttering phrases like 'top of the morning' (which nobody actually says in Ireland!) can be dangerously misleading.

Beneath the general bonhomie, the Irish are much more reticent about exposing their innermost feelings than first impressions might indicate. Not as formal as the English in personal relationships, the Irish are unlikely to bear their souls to anyone other than close friends or family.

Hot Tip: Watch Out for Gossip!

The small size of Ireland means that everybody knows (or thinks they know) everyone else's business. Gossip travels fast! The other side of the coin is that everyone is keen to preserve their individual privacy. Consequently, there often emerges a wonderful contradiction whereby in trying to preserve their own privacy, people are happy to add to the rumour mills to keep the limelight off themselves . . . but like any mill wheel, it just goes round and round!

HOME LIFE AND CHILDREN

Home life in Ireland is much the same as elsewhere in the developed Western world, with the same comforts and facilities which one would expect in Europe or North America.

Visitors from Britain would find the approach more informal than they would be used to. Dropping by, without a prior telephone call, is considered acceptable and informal social events, a gathering over a few drinks in the evenings are not uncommon. Standing on ceremony or dressing up for a call on friends would be seen as precious.

The Irish attitude towards children is akin to that in southern Europe. Children are accepted at social events provided they are not making nuisances of themselves and, even if they do, it would cause less angst than in some other countries. Irish families were relatively large up to recently but Irish fertility rates are dropping fast.

It is also increasingly common for both spouses to work outside the home, so the pattern of family life in Ireland is rapidly becoming much the same as elsewhere in the West, especially among younger people.

ACCENT

Despite its small size, there is a wide variety of regional accents in Ireland, ranging from the melodious in the south to the more clipped in the north. The Dublin accent is also quite distinctive.

Accents vary with class and, for that reason, can be a sensitive subject which the visitor might better avoid unless very sure of his/her ground. Accents are, by and large, a matter of pronunciation: there is no equivalent, for example, of Cockney rhyming slang so that the English-speaking visitor is unlikely to encounter serious comprehension problems.

Parliament building and Garda

SEXUAL MORES

The sexual mores of the younger generation in Ireland probably do not differ from their counterparts elsewhere in the developed world.

It was not always so. Contraceptives have only become freely available in the last twenty years. A referendum in November 1995 narrowly approved the legalization of divorce. Abortion was unintentionally legalized by a constitutional amendment in the 1980s but is not performed in the Republic. (The Irish abortion rate is believed to run at the Western average but Irish women go abroad for this purpose.) Homosexuality is also now legal.

Sexual scandals are not generally a feature of Irish political life: those which so enliven British political life are virtually unknown. However, clerical scandals are quite another matter. In recent years, the country has been agog, firstly with the lurid details of a bishop believed to have fathered a love-child and, more recently, a media priest posthumously claimed to have lived a double sexual life. When an elderly priest died in a gay sauna, two younger priests were on hand to give him the last rites.

Hot Tip: Sex – the Last Taboo . . .

A now-dead member of the *Oireachtas* (Parliament) once famously claimed that there had been no sex in Ireland before television. In a sense he was right: the developing openness about sexuality in Irish life is a by-product of the power of the electronic media in breaking down the old taboos.

5

Politics & Religion

Former President Mary Robinson

Ireland is a parliamentary democracy with a written constitution. This means that fundamental changes (divorce being a recent example) have to be approved by referendum. Parliament (the *Oireachtas*) is elected by a complex but fair proportional representation system. The President, who is directly elected, does not exercise an executive role.

Although remnants of the old Anglo-Irish aristocracy survive, the Irish state, as a Republic, does not confer titles. While visiting members of royal families, including the British, are warmly welcomed, the ethos of the state since its foundation has been austere in relation to pomp and circumstance.

Hot Tip: Friends in the Police!

The Irish police force (*Garda Siochana*, known in popular parlance as 'the Guards') is unarmed. The Guards are well integrated into the community and visitors in need should not hesitate to call on their services.

Talk of politics is a popular Irish pastime but the complexity of the Irish political system with its many nuances, some of which challenge the most rigorous of intellects, is likely to exclude all but the most zealous of outsiders from joining in.

Up to the 1980s, the civil war which followed independence in 1921 formed a basic dividing line in Irish politics. However, that division has faded and, aided by the voting system which militates against overall majorities for any one party, coalitions seem to have replaced single-party government.

The election in 1990 of a liberal woman, Mary Robinson, as President was seen by many as marking a fundamental shift in Irish politics away from conservative stereotypes. She has since been succeeded by another articulate female former lawyer, Mary McAleese.

Irish politics have traditionally lacked the hard ideological edge which has existed elsewhere. There is a high degree of cooperation between the social partners on issues such as wage and income levels.

Bill Clinton's visit to Ireland, November 1995

With the arrival of the peace process, involving all parties north and south of the border, the country's political agenda has inevitably become a major national preoccupation. This was greatly underlined and given a special new dimension as a result of President Clinton's visit at the end of November 1995. Thus, whatever visitors do or say to empathize positively in the desire for a lasting peace will be warmly welcomed.

RELIGION

The Republic of Ireland is overwhelmingly Roman Catholic although its small Protestant minority continues to exercise a marked influence on economic and social life, which as we have seen, has much to do with history.

Relations between the denominations in the Republic, however, have been cordial since independence in 1921. The main Protestant denomination is the Anglican Church of Ireland (generally low-church in orientation). There are also small Jewish and Islamic communities.

Visitors should be warmly welcomed in any place of worship. It is no longer necessary to dress in one's 'Sunday best' and informality is now the general rule; if in doubt, a jacket and tie for males and equivalent for females would ensure that one is not out of place.

Most people in Ireland attend religious services regularly. This means weekly attendance at Mass for Roman Catholics and colourful, quasi-public ceremonies to mark the major liturgical events, such as Easter, Pentecost and the feast of Corpus Christi (17 July). Visitors will probably be struck by the sight of children dressed in full regalia for their 'First Communion'. (The young girls, dressed as miniature brides, are particularly striking for those unfamiliar with the ritual.)

Many aspects of Irish life continue to be organized on denominational lines, especially education. However, the decline in numbers serving in the Roman Catholic priesthood, among other factors, is leading to growing secularization.

Funerals occupy a central part in everyday life. They are public occasions when an entire community gathers to pay tribute to the deceased. It is considered a mark of respect to attend, even if your connection to the deceased is tenuous or indirect.

Irish attitudes towards death in general are quite different from some other Western cultures, especially the English. Mourning in Ireland is public and there is no shame in showing your feelings. You would be expected to commiserate with a friend or acquaintance (including the business world) who has suffered a recent loss.

Hot Tip: Enjoy St Patrick's Day: No Kissing Please!

St Patrick's Day (17 March) is still primarily a religious holiday in Ireland. While some of the razzmatazz which surrounds it in America has been exported back to Ireland in recent years, do not expect green beer or the 'kiss me, I'm Irish!' exuberance of the American experience. A get-together with friends for clubbing or pubbing, is more like the order of the day.

PUBLIC HOLIDAYS IN IRELAND

* = *Variable date*

New Year's Day (1 January)

St Patrick's Day (17 March)

Good Friday (Late March/early April)*

Easter Monday (Late March/early April)*

First Monday in May

First Monday in June

First Monday in August

Last Monday in October

Christmas Day (25 December)

Boxing (St Stephen's) Day (26 December)

Shamrock

6

A Love of the Language

Kissing the Blarney Stone

The Irish are fabled for their linguistic prowess and have produced some of the finest writers in the English language. Names such as W.B. Yeats, James Joyce, George Bernard Shaw, Samuel Beckett and Sean O'Casey are known to lovers of literature the world over.

Hot Tip: The Gift of the 'Blarney'

A gift for the 'blarney' (from the Blarney Stone in County Cork, the kissing of which is supposed to confer a silver tongue) is generally supposed to represent an archetypical Irishman's ability to charm, preferably in a soft brogue.

While there are those, of course, who self-evidently have not been blessed with the 'blarney', there is some truth in the stereotype. Linguistic ability is valued in Ireland and the unbroken line of outstanding Irish playwrights in English from the eighteenth century bears witness to Irish society's love of verbal pyrotechnics.

Since the nineteenth century, however, English has been the language spoken by the great majority of the people in Ireland. North American visitors will find that Irish usage and spelling follow English rather than American forms. At the same time, the growing influence of American English is as evident in Ireland as elsewhere and Americans may find that there is a general understanding of much of their usage ('getting to first base', 'going for broke' and referring to children and other close groups as 'you guys' etc.).

Despite its small size, there is a great deal of regional variation in relation to accent and certain aspects of usage. Despite this, visitors proficient in English should encounter little difficulty in comprehension – whichever part of the country they are in.

Hot Tip: Importance of Understatement

In general, the Irish *do* love language; picturesque phrases and colourful images abound. On the other hand, understatement is also very prevalent. Somebody who is, glaringly, terminally ill might be said to be looking 'a bit shook'. If someone suggests a 'gargle' they mean going for a drink.

Indirectness in speech can represent a delicate linguistic ballet under which uncomfortable truths can be hinted at or propositions advanced with minimal loss of face if rejected. It is important if doing business, especially in more rural areas, that a visitor be tuned in to these subtleties.

As noted earlier (see 'Accent' in Ch. 4), and just like England, accent in Ireland is pregnant with class and other resonances and, as a general rule of thumb, it is better to avoid comment on accent unless one is very sure of one's ground.

The Gaelic language, generally called Irish, a Celtic language spoken by the mass of the people until the early nineteenth century, is now the first language of a small minority, mostly concentrated on the western seaboard.

Overall, around 2% of the population (about 60,000 people) speak Irish as a first language. On the other hand, over a million people, or almost one-third of the population of the Republic, claim proficiency in the language.

No longer compulsory, Irish is still learned by the vast majority of children at school. Even if they do not use it in everyday life, many Irish people retain an attachment to the language and certain Irish words and phrases still flavour everyday speech in English. A glossary of some of the more common ones has been included at the end of this chapter.

Hot Tip: Reward for Effort!

It would not be expected of foreigners that they should understand any Irish but the visitor who does make even a minimal effort in this direction (for example, by being aware that the Prime Minister is known by his title of *Taoiseach*, pronounced 'Teeshock') will gain disproportionately in goodwill.

Even being aware that there is an Irish language which is not merely a variation of English, and which is the repository of a marvellous literary tradition, will definitely be appreciated.

Irish lesson

COMMON GREETINGS/SAYINGS IN IRISH

There are many greetings and responses in the Irish language. These vary even depending on the dialect. Here are a few examples:

Dia duit	(Lit. God to you)
Dia is Muire duit	(Lit. God and Mary to you)
Go mbeannaí Dia duit	May God bless you
Go mbeannaí Dia is Muire duit	May God and Mary bless you
Bail ó Dhia ort	The blessing of God on you
Bail ó Dhia is Muir duit	The blessing of God and Mary on you
Go raibh maith agat	Thanks (Lit. May there be good at you)
Go dtaga do íocht	May thy kingdom come
Nár laga Dia do lámh	May God not weaken your hand
Gura slán and scéalaí	May the bearer of the news be safe
Gurab amhlaidh duit	The same to you
Tá fáilte romhat	You are welcome
Conas atá tú?	How are you?
Tá mé go maith	I'm doing well
An bhfuil aon rud úr ag dul?	What's new?
Slán leat	Good bye (said to one going)

Slán agat	Good bye (said to one remaining)
Sláinte chugat	Good health to you
Gabhaim pardún agat	I beg your pardon
Gabh mo leithscéal	Pardon me (Lit. Accept my excuse)
Más é do thoil é	If you please
Le do thoil	Please
Saol fada chugat	Long life to you

'*Gurab amhlaidh duit*' is a common answer to the following greetings:

Oíche mhaith duit	Good night
Codlah sámh duit	A pleasant sleep
Mollaig shona duit	Happy Christmas
Athbhliain faoi mhaise duit	A prosperous New Year

Terms of Endearment

a ghrá
a rún
a stór
a thaisce   } my dear darling/love/treasure
a chroí
a chuisle

muirnín
leannán   } sweetheart
céadsearc

a ghrá/ mo chroí   love of my heart!

7

Business Matters

Traditional and new industry

The Irish economy has two distinct sectors: the indigenous, much of which is still related to the long-established strengths of the economy in agriculture and the traditional industries; and, the newer, largely high-tech, sector developed mostly by foreign capital.

This distinction is not as pronounced as it used to be, with the emergence of indigenous entrepreneurs in the newer sectors. Ireland is the second largest exporter of computer software in the world, after the USA, and attracts 25% of all investment in electronics in the European Union.

As the British, Americans and Germans are among the largest investors in Ireland, visiting businessmen should not find dealing with their Irish counterparts in the foreign-funded areas of the economy fundamentally different from elsewhere in the developed West. Even in the traditional industries, where the approach a generation ago might have been much more relaxed, the law of the bottom line applies as ruthlessly as anywhere else. After all, the old sectors of the economy have had to survive the global forces which have weeded out so many of the sunset industries in the last twenty years.

Ireland has embraced the possibilities which membership of the European Union has provided to diversify its trading pattern away from an over-dependence on the British market, and is a founding member of the new European currency, the Euro.

Even so, the human touch remains vitally important in Ireland and the old rural tradition of indirectness still survives. Aggressive sales techniques are unlikely to be appreciated, especially in country areas. It is far better to take things slowly and allow your professional relationship to develop as your Irish interlocutor comes to know and trust you.

The ability to relax and enjoy whatever entertainment is provided is important; ostentatious self-importance will win you few friends. A visiting businessman might well be taken to a nightclub after dinner where the revelry could continue until the wee small hours. Pubs where music is performed, especially of the traditional variety (see Ch.10), are a common feature of Irish life and visitors are often taken along.

Hot Tip: Relax With a Song!

Shyness or reticence in public is understood but the visitor who, when invited on a social occasion, can give a rendition of a song or ballad from their own culture will certainly be appreciated. And it will help in establishing a relaxed personal relationship with your Irish host or hostess which will definitely be an advantage when it comes to the core business decisions.

Ireland's remarkable economic performance in recent years has been underpinned by a 'Programme for Competitiveness and Work', essentially a broad 'social contract' between the major social partners, which has helped make the trade (US 'labor') unions associates rather than adversaries in their relationship with capital. Visitors dealing with unions should seek partnership in the first instance.

Punctuality is recommended for business appointments as the old *laissez-faire* attitudes are being squeezed out of Irish economic life. If your Irish counterparts are serious about doing business with you then they will be punctual and will expect the same from you.

The best approach to confirmation of business appointments is probably a combination of the English (appointments in essence do not need confirmation) and the American (a sequence of confirmations can lead up to the event itself) approaches: the appointment could be confirmed by letter or fax when made (especially if coming from abroad) and followed up with a telephone call the day before.

Suits still tend to be the norm for business or professional activity and, unless your host specifies casual dress, for dinner parties as well. Entry to some night clubs (those dealing with a more mature clientele) will be facilitated by wearing a jacket and tie. Some upmarket restaurants might expect similar attire.

The Irish telecommunications network is highly digitized so that visiting businessmen should have no difficulty with using portable computers, modems or cellular phones (provided, of course, that they are designed for international use). Americans should be aware that local calls are charged. There are a number of Internet providers.

Most businesses in Ireland operate a forty-hour, five-day week. Retail outlets are generally open from 9–9.30am to 5.30–6pm, Monday to Saturday, depending on the type of business carried on. In the cities especially, there has been a growth of late-opening mini-supermarkets catering to the increasing number of people who operate outside conventional working hours.

Hot Tip: You Can Enjoy Yourself on Sundays!

The proliferation of the fast-food culture, as ubiquitous as in any other part of the West, means that you can eat cheaply most hours of the day or night. Acquiring the necessities of life on a Sunday is not a problem as the Irish do not have a rigid Sabbatarian culture (Gaelic games, for example, are played on Sundays).

'Suits are the norm. . .'

8

The Sporting Life

Hurling

With the growth of corporate entertainment, visitors, especially business people, are increasingly likely to find themselves invited to sports events such as rugby internationals and race meetings.

Japanese or American visitors should note that involvement in horse-racing confers high status in Ireland and betting on the outcome is acceptable at all levels of society.

The casual visitor need not worry unduly about dress at sports events but the recipients of hospitality should dress fairly formally. A suit or sports jacket, with stout shoes such as brogues, would be appropriate for men, while the women will find that they need to dress with a degree of fashion-consciousness not to be out of place with their Irish counterparts. (For those with a budget to match, wearing an outfit from an internationally-recognized Irish designer, such as Paul Costello, would be a definite plus!)

Many major sporting events are tied in with formal social occasions such as a ball at which a dinner-jacket for men and equivalent dress for women is an absolute requirement. Invitees should check this point carefully in advance.

The most popular sports in Ireland are the Gaelic games of football and hurling. Croke Park, near Dublin, the headquarters of Gaelic games, is being rebuilt as an 80,000-plus stadium with lavish corporate entertainment facilities, so it is likely that an increasing number of business and other visitors will be invited to major games there in the future. Irish sporting crowds are good-natured and free from violent behaviour.

Hot Tip: Rules of the Irish Games: Gaelic Football & Hurling

Understanding the rudiments of Gaelic football and hurling is quite easy. Both feature fifteen players and scoring is represented by putting the ball between rugby-style uprights, over the crossbar for one point and under for a goal (three points).

Both games demand high levels of skill and athleticism, of which visitors might attempt intelligent appreciation. Hurling, played with sticks and a small, hard leather ball, is one of the fastest field games in the world and is referred to in the early Irish sagas.

Sport is an excellent way to meet the Irish and to mix in an unselfconscious way. The number of golf courses is, in relation to the size of the population, among the highest in the world and other participation sports, like tennis, are well catered for. Dress code for these sports is much the same as in Britain or America.

The lush plains of some of the countryside around Dublin are ideally suited to the breeding of horses and the horsey world generally – the preserve of the Anglo-Irish in the old days – now brings together the rural and urban élites as well as ordinary people intent on having a good time.

Major sporting occasions tend to become great national events in Ireland. Rugby, for example, is, in the ordinary course of events, a minority sport, largely confined to the white-collar occupations; when, however, Ireland are playing an international, the entire country switches on to watch.

This effect is even more dramatic in the case of soccer, particularly now that the national team enjoyed a golden period of success under the management of the Englishman, Jack Charlton who retired in January 1996.

Dublin's main thoroughfares can be deserted as most of the population stays in to watch key international matches. Similarly, the whole country will take a passing interest in, and maybe gamble a few pounds on, high-profile horse races. The Dublin Horse Show is a major event in the equestrian calendar.

'Horse-racing confers high status in Ireland'

9

Food & Eating Out

'. . .the synergic coupling of oysters and Guinness'

The Irish diet is broadly similar to that of Britain although continental Europe has exercised an increasing influence over the last twenty years and, like Britain, has done much to bring about a new focus on quality, choice and service. (Cookery books are consistently among the top ten best-sellers.)

Forms of meals vary by social class, occasion and the urban/rural divide. The traditional rural form (Ireland, as already noted, was predominantly rural until a generation or so ago) was a hearty breakfast, the main meal of 'meat and two veg' (i.e. vegetables) in the middle of the day and 'tea', a less substantial meal, at about 6 pm in the evening.

With the growth of urbanization and health consciousness, the fried breakfast, once so popular, is increasingly less common among the growing middle class. The norm is now more likely to be a light breakfast, followed by a sandwich lunch or its equivalent, and dinner or supper in the evening.

Afternoon tea has never occupied the place in Irish life that it has in England but it survives in hotels especially and can be an excellent way for the visitor to sample the more exclusive establishments, usually at reasonable cost.

Nothing symbolizes the transformation of Irish life in the last twenty years more than the enormous growth of restaurants and eating establishments of all kinds. In Dublin particularly it is now possible to sample many of the world's cuisines to a variety of costs and standards. Cafes, modelled on their continental European equivalents, are mushrooming in urban areas throughout the country, contributing to the evolution of a whole new life-style.

Hot Tip: Irish Generosity

Irish portions of food tend towards the generous (generosity – in Irish *flathuail* – is a much-admired trait in Irish life), even in international hotels but no offence will be taken if a surplus remains uneaten.

Continental-style cafes. . . 'mushrooming in urban areas'

Service is probably somewhere between the leisurely which can characterize continental Europe and the extreme rapidity of North America. Americans, in particular, might need to be aware that an aggressive attitude towards speed of service and the price-quality ratio, while theoretically justified, might cause resentment. The Irish themselves, while they may grumble privately, tend to suffer in silence.

Hot Tip: Tipping is Expected

Tipping is expected in hotels and restaurants with 10–15% being the norm. The iniquitous practice of adding a fixed percentage charge to the bill (US 'check') has been introduced in some establishments, sometimes leaving the customer with no option except to add even more of a tip!

While Ireland has not evolved as comprehensive a cuisine as, say, France or Italy, it does have distinctive foods which the visitor should sample. Traditional dishes such as 'boxty' (a potato pancake, using both mashed and ordinary boiled potatoes, fried in bacon fat) or 'colcannon' (a type of mashed, creamed potato incorporating cabbage and onion, usually served on Halloween, 31 October) are well worth seeking out and would form excellent conversation pieces with Irish hosts, not all of whom might be familiar with them!

Seafood is a particular Irish speciality and many pubs offer the synergic coupling of oysters and Guinness (or other brands of black beer ('stout')), a relatively cheap and excellent way to get a 'taste of Ireland'.

Traditional Irish breakfasts are another inexpensive way of sampling some distinctive tastes, especially white and black puddings (made from pig's blood). Some of the best breakfasts are provided by farmhouses (an excellent way to come close to the real Ireland), although not recommended for cholesterol-watchers!

Table manners in Ireland follow the English pattern of holding the knife in the right hand and the fork in the left; the American practice of changing the fork over to the right hand to eat with, after the food has been cut up, is not followed. It is best to eat with the mouth closed – loud noises when eating, a sign of appreciation in some cultures, are to be avoided in polite society!

10

The Irish Pub

'The Pub. . .an important focus of Irish social life'

The pub is an important focus of Irish social life. It is an egalitarian place where all classes and nationalities can mingle and enjoy the art of conversation over a few drinks. There is an easiness, a sense of bonhomie which – quite apart from the drink – can prove intoxicating.

A foreigner can be expected to arouse friendly curiosity and, if he or she so desires, be drawn into conversation, although the record numbers of tourists who have been visiting during the last decade, together with high levels of immigration, have lessened somewhat the curiosity value of unfamiliar faces. . .

Hot Tip: The Irish Don't Drink — That Much!

Nobody works harder to promote an image of wild excess surrounding Irish pub culture than the Irish themselves. However, the sober statistics tell another story: the Irish are among the most modest consumers of alcohol in the developed world!

There are a number of reasons for this. One is the very high rate of total abstinence from alcohol in Ireland. A visitor need never therefore feel under any compulsion to drink if he or she does not wish to do so.

Also, the Irish do not as a rule drink with their meals. A visitor should remember that the person he is meeting in a pub in the evening is unlikely to have drunk anything so far that day and to have had a substantial meal as padding.

Another factor which the unwary visitor should take into account is the inflating effect which a propensity to dramatization can have on the prodigious amounts allegedly consumed by their interlocutor the previous night. (Division by a factor of anything up to five can often be in order!)

The Irish are a naturally generous people and, although the 'round' system (buying a drink for all in your company) is nothing like as prevalent as it was a generation ago, it is still an important fact of pub culture. If you have accepted a drink from an individual or as part of a round, you should reciprocate. No one will say anything if you do not but they may not be as pleased to see you the following evening! Similarly, if you are smoking, you should offer the packet around to your companions (again, no comment will be passed if you decide not to; you will simply come across as mildly anti-social).

In the last thirty years Irish pubs have been transformed from essentially male-dominated drinking haunts (the 'snugs', partitioned-off areas to which women were confined in the old days, can still be seen – though no longer used! – in some of the older pubs) where food was an afterthought (if it was served at all) to social centres where both sexes are equally welcome; excellent and reasonably-priced food is generally available, especially at lunch-time.

There has also been a significant development of cafes in Ireland, some of which serve both alcohol as well as coffee, tea and light food.

There is a wide variety of Irish pubs, reflecting the range of the clientele and the diversity of their interests. In some rural pubs, Gaelic games may be the main topic of conversation while one Dublin pub has given its name to a school of economics.

Hot Tip: Enjoy the Music!

Many pubs, both rural and urban, are home to musical expression of all kinds, especially Irish traditional. Very often there is no charge for these '*seisiuns*' (musical happenings) and a visitor may find outstanding 'name' musicians jamming anonymously in a pub, sometimes at a quieter time, like Sunday morning. A visitor with sufficient musical skill would generally always be welcome to join in.

Licensing laws in Ireland are broadly similar to those in England and visiting Americans or continental Europeans might regard them as restrictive. Pubs close at 11.30pm in the summer and at 11pm in the winter. Guests in hotels can obtain alcoholic drinks after that from room-service or the night porter.

A pub '*seisiun*'

Hot Tip: No Pub Tips!

There is no tipping in Irish pubs except, possibly, where you are seated at a table and availing of service to bring you drinks (even here it is not necessary although it will be appreciated). The English practice of offering the bar staff a drink is not widespread.

During the quieter periods, bar patrons may sit at the bar or around tables but during the busy period from 9pm onwards, it is perfectly normal to stand.

CHOICE OF DRINKS

Unlike some other European countries – England and Belgium, for example – Ireland does not produce a great variety of local ales or beers although there are some well worth sampling. In any event, they are under increasing pressure from a growing variety of imports.

Guinness, a brand of dark beer called 'stout' or 'porter' at home and synonymous with Ireland around the world, is as close as one can get to a national drink. Other brands of stout, such as Beamish or Murphy's have devoted followings, particularly in specific local areas, such as Cork, the second largest city in the south.

The old-fashioned luke-warm draught beers drawn by hand from wooden barrels, still so much a feature of English pubs, have been elbowed out by the ubiquitous metal, gas/pressurized cask, with the beers served chilled. Die-hard Guinness loyalists claim, rightly, that their beloved potion tastes best at room temperature but it is increasingly difficult to find pubs which serve it that way.

Draught beer in Ireland is served in pint (something over half a litre) and half-pint (colloquially called a 'glass') measures.

Hot Tip: Discover Irish 'Whiskey'

The Irish take pride in having invented whiskey (note the extra 'e' over Scotch), a corruption of the Gaelic *uisce beatha*, translated as 'the water of life'. Irish whiskey is distinctive and aficionados hold Scotch in contempt. Ordering Irish whiskey rather than Scotch will gain brownie points for visitors.

Beware! Irish spirit measures are larger than their English counterparts and the unwary can easily come to grief. A measure of whiskey consumed after a pint of beer is called a 'chaser'; hardened drinkers continue alternating the two (clearly a practice with potential for disaster, for the unseasoned drinker especially).

The Irish drinking toast is '*slainte!*' (literally meaning 'health'), the equivalent of the English 'cheers!'

Pubs are the epicentre of that quintessentially Irish but elusive concept, the *craic*. Pronounced 'crack' like, but unrelated to, the deadly narcotic

(American visitors have, from time to time, made appalled assumptions about what was in store for them!), *craic* is a virtually untranslatable word which applies to having a good time in Ireland, when the booze flows, the music is good and the conversation sparkles; dancing may be involved.

IRELAND'S TRADITIONAL MUSIC

Ireland retains a wonderful tradition of indigenous music, both vocal and instrumental, which has been revitalized by cross-pollination with rock and other outside influences in the last thirty years.

Making music

TRADITIONAL MUSICAL INSTRUMENTS

Sean-nos singing is an unaccompanied and highly ornamented form. Traditional Irish music features a number of distinctive instruments, including:

Uilleann (Union) pipes: played seated, the piper inflates the bag by operating a bellows with one arm, and maintains pressure on the bag with the other arm.

Bodhran: a goatskin drum used widely in Irish music (a famous Irish entertainer once remarked that you were Irish if the bodhran sent shivers down your spine!).

Harp: Harping is an ancient tradition in Ireland (it is the national symbol) and was closely tied to the old aristocracy and 'high' culture.

Percussion: *Bones* (usually short wooden sticks or cow rib bones, clicked against each other, a little like castanets) and *spoons* are sometimes used to provide accompaniment. In Northern Ireland, the gigantic Lambeg drums are a symbol of the Orange (unionist) musical tradition.

Some other instruments which feature prominently in Irish music are the fiddle (exactly the same as a violin), flutes (mainly the 'simple-system' flute with six holes and up to eight keys), the 'tin' or 'penny' whistle (a simple metal tube, with six holes and a mouthpiece like a recorder, and a range of about two octaves), and accordions of various kinds (the melodeon is a simple single-action accordion).

11

Out & About

Typical Irish landscape

CLOTHING

Rain-proof outer clothing and/or an umbrella are fundamental hedges against the vagaries of Ireland's moist and temperate climate. It does rain a lot in Ireland. (On the other hand, you do not spend six months of the year up to your knees in snow or deal with a mosquito-infested summer.)

Ireland's mild climate means that, once protected against the rain, you can participate in outdoor activities all year round. Otherwise, Irish clothing follows the norms of most of the rest of the Western world.

If you have been invited to stay in a country house, including the grand Anglo-Irish variety, good warm clothing – tweeds for example – is a useful precaution. Even on a summer trip, warm casual clothes, including a jumper, should be packed.

Many visitors like to stock up on distinctive Irish clothing – Aran sweaters and the like – when in Ireland. By all means wear them while in the country but be careful not to overdo it: a visitor who wears a lot of traditional clothing might be the subject of a certain sly humour.

Waterford Glass craftsman

THE WONDERS OF IRELAND

Beautiful scenery is to be found all over Ireland and, as a relatively small country, a visitor with a car should be able to cover most of it in a few weeks. A visitor landing in Dublin might head south to Cork, the second city of Ireland, which has a unique atmosphere of its own.

West Cork and Kerry, in the southeast, are renowned for their rugged beauty while, to the north of the river Shannon lies the county of Clare, with the unique landscape of the rocky Burren country. Galway, steeped in history, is the major city of the west coast.

The landscape of Sligo, further north, has been immortalized in the poems of W.B. Yeats. Donegal, to the northwest, is one of the most distinctively beautiful counties in the country.

There are many sights to be investigated by the visitor: the Rock of Cashel, with its medieval ecclesiastical architecture perched on a great rock; Blarney Castle where kissing the Blarney Stone confers the 'gift of the gab' (fluent speech); the cliffs of Moher in county Clare; the lakes of Killarney, etc., but the real charm of Ireland is the slow exploration of a countryside of great variety and constant ability to surprise.

Among the most popular tourist attractions in the Republic of Ireland are: the Rock of Cashel (Co Tipperary); Kilkenny Castle (Kilkenny city); Clonmacnois (Co Offaly; the remains of a medieval monastic settlement); Glendalough (Co Wicklow; also a monastic settlement); Kilmainham Gaol (Dublin; nineteenth century prison buildings where the 1916 leaders were executed); Illnacullin – Garinish Island (Co Cork); Connemara National Park (Co Galway); Glenveagh Castle and National Park (Co Donegal); Cahir Castle (Co Tipperary); and, John F. Kennedy Park (Co Wexford).

GETTING PLUGGED IN

The Irish electrical system operates on 220volts/ 50cycles. Although there is a small voltage difference with the UK system, UK appliances should work without difficulty; the sockets and plugs are the same. Visitors from continental Europe will find that their appliances will also work on Ireland's similar power supply but they will need adaptors to cope with different plugs/ sockets. North American visitors will need adaptors both for the different voltage/cycles and plugs/sockets.

Ireland is well provided with newspapers, which carry a good mix of national and international news. *The Irish Times*, regarded as the main quality daily (but not the largest circulation: that honour belongs to the *Irish Independent*, also a quality broadsheet) is transmitted daily on the Internet.

The British newspapers are available throughout the country from early in the morning on the day of issue. The British tabloids, which find a voracious audience among the less educated, print Irish editions (sometimes with unintentionally hilarious results, as when gung-ho denunciations of Ireland or its people are muted or even reversed for the Irish readership).

In addition to the television channels of RTE, the national radio and television network (roughly the same as the BBC in Britain or CBC in Canada), an extensive cable network distributes four British television channels and twelve satellite channels. This penetration will increase when a microwave system extends this service to rural areas.

TRAVEL

Irish taxis can be a means, not only of transport, but also of education, particularly on the burning issues of the day. For many people, on their way in from the airport, the taxi driver will be their first encounter with the irreverent, opinionated, garrulous Dublin cabbie. If you wish to sit stiffly, shrouding yourself in executive privilege, he will not mind but you may be the loser.

Hot Tip: How to Find a Cab

Taxis in urban areas operate from ranks or by telephone call: they do not cruise the streets as they might in, say, New York or London. Because of the cost of cars, hiring a car in Ireland is expensive by English or American standards.

Dublin's 'fair city'

The train network, connecting the main towns and cities, can be a fast, cheap and reliable way of getting around (though not to more remote locations). The bus service, too, can be useful. (Foreigners puzzled by the seemingly ubiquitous destination, *An Lar*, on Dublin buses should be aware that it is simply the Irish for the city centre.)

For those with deeper pockets, it is possible to get around the country (by both plane and helicopter) using the regional airports at Donegal, Galway, Kerry, Sligo and Waterford.

12

The Diaspora

There is probably no other people in the world for whom emigration has been more important than the Irish, although this trend has been reversed in recent years, with net immigration now running at around 50,000 per year. The result is that there are many more people of Irish descent around the world than live in the island of Ireland.

Worldwide, the total number of people of Irish descent is estimated at over 60 million; in the United States over 40 million claim Irish descent.

Irish-Americans have been active in all facets of American life and distinguished Americans of Irish descent include Presidents Kennedy, Nixon and Reagan. Canada has also become home to many Irish emigrants: in the 1860s, over 20% of the population was of Irish descent. Up to 30% of the Australian population is of Irish descent, making it the most 'Irish' place in the world outside Ireland! 15% of New Zealand's population is estimated as being of Irish descent.

Many Irish people also played roles in the development of Latin America in the nineteenth century and large numbers settled in Argentina where there is an ethnic Irish population of around 300,000. In Britain today, there are up to one million people of Irish birth and further millions of Irish descent (precise statistics are not available but the figure could be as high as five million).

Irish emigration can be seen in three waves: the missionary effort of the early medieval Christian church; the flight of the Roman Catholic nobility in the seventeenth century; and, the mass emigration since the great famine of the mid-nineteenth century.

The Scots-Irish emigration, from Northern Ireland, took place earlier and while it is now less distinctive, it produced its share of US Presidents and other outstanding achievers.

Many people are aware (as noted above) that up to 21 US Presidents have been of Irish descent, but few know that three British Prime Ministers were born in Dublin (including the Duke of Wellington who, when reminded of his origins, replied that being born in a stable did not make one a horse!).

Wellington, indeed, was one of many out-standing British soldiers of Irish birth or descent: these included Lord Kitchener, Earl Alexander of Tunis, Field Marshall Montgomery, Field Marshall Alanbrooke, Lawrence of Arabia, and Rear-Admiral Charles David Lucas, the first recipient of the Victoria Cross.

The growth of communications is facilitating the re-establishment of contact between these communities around the world and the people of Ireland. In the United States, the political weight of the Irish ethnic population is an important factor in the search for a political settlement covering the islands of Britain and Ireland.

US Presidents Kennedy, Reagan & Nixon

Further Reading

Beckett, J C, *The Making of Modern Ireland*, London, 1981

Brennan, E (Ed), *Heritage: A Visitor's Guide*, Dublin, 1990

Haughton, J P (Ed), *Atlas of Ireland*, Dublin, 1979

Kennedy & Gillispie (Eds), *Ireland: Art into History*, Dublin, 1994

Mitchell, G F, *The Shell Guide to Reading the Irish Language*, Dublin, 1986

Moody, T W & Martin, F X, *The Course of Irish History*, Dublin, 1994

O'Canainn, T, *Traditional Music in Ireland*, 1994

Williams, S E & Forde, P K, *The Irish Literary Tradition*, 1992

Irish Words Used in This Book

For a full listing of Common Greetings and Sayings in Irish, see pages 47-48. Other Irish words used elsewhere in the text are:-

an lar, 75	city centre
bodhran, 68	goatskin drum
craic, 66	'having a good time'
flathuail, 58	generosity

Facts About Ireland

The population of Ireland is approximately 3.6 million and very young, with some 41% under the age of twenty-five and 24% under fifteen. Significantly, in recent years immigration has increased to a point which generates a net inflow (15000 in 1997 – the highest such figure since the 1970s).

Climate

The warmer waters from the Gulf Stream together with the prevailing southwesterly winds from the Atlantic combine to generate a wet but pleasant climate, with temperatures much the same over the whole of the island of Ireland, the warmest mean summer temperatures being in July and August of between 14C and 16C, and between 4C and 7C in the coldest months of January and February. The sunniest months are usually May and June.

Ireland was separated from the European mainland after the last Ice Age. As a result, the island has a smaller range of flora and fauna than is found elsewhere in Europe. In the Burren (Co. Clare), for example, Arctic-Alpine plants survive from the last glaciation, and Ireland's famous bogs host a large variety of bog-moss species together with heather and sedges.

For those who need to know, Ireland is the best place to be on the planet to avoid earthquakes since no epicentre has ever been found there.

In Ireland, traffic drives on the left. The national airline is Aer Lingus (5.3 million passengers in 1997); Ryanair is the privately-owned Irish airline (4 million passengers in 1997).

The introduction of Christianity in the fifth century AD is traditionally credited to St Patrick, though there is evidence that there were Christians on the island before his arrival.

Ireland never experienced the barbarian invasions of the early medieval period and, partly as a result, the sixth and seventh centuries saw a flowering of Irish art, learning and culture centring on the Irish monasteries. The eighth-century *Book of Kells* (exhibited at Trinity College, Dublin) is an excellent example of the art of this period. (See example on p.94.) Irish monks also established centres of learning and Christianity in many parts of Europe in the period before 800AD.

The Literary Tradition

By the sixth century BC, waves of Celtic invaders from Europe began to reach Ireland, and although never unified politically by the Celts, they did generate a cultural and linguistic unity. Written literature in Old Irish dates from this period. Heroic sagas depict the deeds of the mythic warriors *Cu Chulainn* and *Fionn*; lyrical and conventional poetry also survive from that time.

During the early modern period (1250-1650), secular schools trained poets (filidh) to compose elaborate verse. When the Gaelic order ended in the the seventeenth century, the Irish poets lost their patrons and their bardic literature was displaced. This gave rise to extensive popular poetic literature. At the same time, Irish prose writers shifted their emphasis from recounting the deeds of ancient warriors to preserving the record of Gaelic civilization.

Among the first Anglo-Irish writers to achieve success were the satirist, Jonathan Swift (1667-1747), author of *Gulliver's Travels* (1726), the political thinker, Edmund Burke (1729-97), and the dramatists, Oliver Goldsmith (1728-74) and Richard Brinsley Sheridan (1751-1816). Building on that tradition, Oscar Wilde (1854-1900) and George Bernard Shaw (1856-1950) also wrote major dramas for the English stage. Shaw won the Nobel Prize in 1925.

William Butler Yeats (1865-1939), whose work inspired the modern renaissance in Irish writing, was awarded the Nobel Prize in 1923.

See also Ch.6.

Ireland has two Houses of Parliament, known as *Dail Eireann* (House of Representatives) and *Seanad* (Senate). The *Dail* has 166 members who are elected on a system of proportional representation. The head of the government is the *Taoiseach* (Prime Minister). The *Seanad* has 60 members, eleven of whom are nominated by the *Taoiseach*, while the rest are elected from a number of vocational panels by the graduates of universities.

The Irish police force, *An Carda Siochana*, are unarmed.

The Irish telecommunications system is one of the most advanced in Europe. There are some 83 telephone lines per 100 households. The international network is 100% digital, and the digital mobile phone network serves over 95% of the population.

The Economy

In 1997, exports accounted for 73% of GDP, with the main areas of growth being computers and electrical machinery, as well as chemicals and pharmaceuticals. The principal destinations for Ireland's exports are: UK 24.3%, Germany 12.5%, the US 11.4% and France 7.9%.

Agriculture accounts for 7% of GDP, 10.3% of total employment, and agricultural products around 9% of exports. Tourism, on the other hand, is one of Ireland's fastest growing industries. Overseas visitor numbers have grown from 2.3 million in 1988 to just over 5 million in 1997; of these 57% came from Britain and 16% from North America.

The period of compulsory education is from six to fifteen. After primary education, the second-level sector comprises secondary, vocational, community and comprehensive schools, all publicly-aided. Of these, some 450 are secondary schools, accounting for 60% of the post-primary students. These schools are privately owned and managed. Most are managed by religious orders, the rest by boards of governors or by individuals. The State meets around 95% of the cost of teacher's salaries.

Ireland has four universities: the University of Dublin (Trinity College), the National University of Ireland (NUI), the University of Limerick and Dublin City University.

Irish is the country's first official language and is part of the Celtic family of languages, closely related to Scottish Gaelic, Welsh and Breton. Most people spoke Irish until the early nineteenth century, but by 1891 over 85% spoke only English.

Some Unusual Irish Firsts

- The British Museum was founded by Sir Hans Sloane (1660-1753), born in Co.Down; Sloane Square in London is named after him.

- John Joly (1857-1933), Professor of Geology at Trinity College, Dublin, developed the first practical system of colour photography.

- John R. Gregg, from Monaghan (1876-1948) invented shorthand.

- The world's first submarine was invented by John Philip Holland (1841-1914), an Irish ex-Christian Brother.

- The world's first tank, used at the battle of the Somme in 1916, was co-designed by the Dubliner, Walter Gordon Wilson (1874-1957).

- Ireland's first cinema was opened in Dublin by James Joyce in 1909. Ireland has the highest rate of cinema attendance in Europe.

Partly as a result of the Irish cultural revival reinforced by the country's remarkable economic revival, which has been evident since the mid-1980s, increasing numbers of people (around 30%) claim to have some knowledge of Irish.

By 1997 Ireland boasted the highest level of job creation in the industrialized world.

Old Irish, Ireland's vernacular when the historical period began in the sixth century is the earliest variant of the Celtic languages; it is also the earliest of European languages north of the Alps in which extensive writings are extant. The Gaelic alphabet of 17 letters was developed from Latin orthography in the sixth century.

Irish Folklore

Much of Irish lore centres on the patron-saints of the various localities. These saints, historical personages from the early centuries of Irish Christianity, are portrayed in legend as miracle-workers who used their sacred power to banish monsters, cure illnesses, and provide food for the people in time of need.

Holy wells, dedicated to individual saints, are still frequented on their feast-days in many areas; people pray at these wells for relief from different kinds of physical and mental distress. Most celebrated are the national saint, St.Patrick; the great founder of monasteries, Colm Cille; and the ubiquitous Brighid who, as protectress of farming and livestock, preserves many of the attributes of the ancient earth goddess.

Irish Fairy Lore

Ireland is also famous for its fairy lore, which contains vestiges of pre-Christian traditions. In Irish, fairies are known as *sí*, a word which originally designated a mound or tumulus. The Irish fairies can be connected with the early Celtic beliefs of how the dead live on as a dazzling community in their burial chambers.

Some Traditional Irish Songs

THE CROPPY BOY

1. 'Twas early, early in the spring
   The birds did whistle and sweetly sing
   Changing their notes from tree to tree
   And the song they sang was 'Old Ireland Free'

2. 'Twas early, early in the night
   The yeoman cavalry gave me a fright
   The yeoman cavalry was my downfall
   And taken was I by the Lord Cornwall

3. 'Twas in the guard-house where I was laid
   And in the parlour where I was tried
   My sentence passed and my courage low
   When to Dungannon I was forced to go

4. As I was passing my father's door
   My brother William stood at the door
   My agèd father stood there also
   My tender mother her hair she tore

5. As I was going up Wexford Street
   My own first cousin I chanced to meet
   My own first cousin did me betray
   And for one bare guinea swore my life away

6. As I was going up Wexford Hill
   Who could blame me to cry my fill?
   I looked behind and I looked before
   My agèd mother I shall see no more

7. As I was mounted on the scaffold high
   My agèd father was standing by
   My agèd father did me deny
   And the name he gave me was the Croppy Boy

8. It was in Dungannon this young man died
   And in Dungannon his body lies
   And you good people that do pass by
   Oh shed a tear for the Croppy Boy

— o —

DANNY BOY
(Londonderry Air)

1. Oh Danny Boy the pipes, the pipes are calling
   From glen to glen, and down the mountain side
   The summer's gone, and all the roses falling
   'Tis you, 'tis you must go, and I must bide.
   But come ye back when summer's in the meadow
   Or when the valley's hushed and white with snow
   'Tis I'll be there in sunshine or in shadow
   Oh, Danny Boy, oh Danny Boy I love you so

2. And when ye come, and all the flowers are dying
   If I am dead, as dead I well may be
   You'll come and find the place where I am lying
   And kneel and say an 'Ave' there for me.
   And I shall hear though soft you tread above me
   And all my grave will warmer, sweeter be
   If you will bend and tell me that you love me
   Then I shall sleep in peace until you come to me

— o —

I'LL TAKE YOU HOME AGAIN, KATHLEEN

1. I'll take you home again Kathleen
   Across the ocean wild and wide
   To where your heart has ever been
   Since first you were my bonny bride.
   The Roses have all left your cheek
   I've watched them fade away and die
   Your voice is sad when e'er you speak
   And tears bedim your loving eyes
     Oh! I will take you back Kathleen
     To where your heart will feel no pain
     And when the fields are fresh and green
     I'll take you to your home again

2. I know you love me Kathleen dear
   Your heart was ever fond and true
   I always feel when you are near
   That life holds nothing dear but you.
   The smiles that once you gave to me
   I scarcely ever see them now
   Though many, many times I see
   A darkening shadow on your brow.
     Oh! I will take you back Kathleen. . .

3. To that dear home beyond the sea
   My Kathleen shall again return
   And when thy old friends welcome thee
   Thy loving heart will cease to yearn.
   Where laughs the little silver stream
   Beside your master's humble cot
   And brightest rays of sunshine gleam
   There all your grief will be forgot.
     Oh! I will take you back Kathleen. . .

— o —

THE IRISH ROVER

1. In the year of Our Lord, eighteen hundred and six
   We set sail from the coal quay of Cork.
   We were sailing away with a cargo of bricks
   For the grand city hall in New York.
   We'd an elegant craft, it was rigged fore and aft
   And how the trade winds drove her.
   She had twenty-three masts, and she stood several
   blasts
   And they called her the Irish Rover.

2. There was Barney Magee from the banks of the Lee
   There was Hogan from County Tyrone
   There was Johnny McGurk who was scared stiff of
   work
   And a chap from Westmeath named Malone.
   There was Slugger O'Toole who drank as a rule
   And fighting Bill Tracy from Dover
   And your man Mick McCann from the banks of the
   Bann
   Was the skipper on the Irish Rover

3. We had one million bags of the best Sligo rags
   We had two million barrels of bone
   We had three million bales of old nanny goats' tails
   We had four million barrels of stone.
   We had five million hogs and six million dogs
   And seven million barrels of porter
   We had eight million sides of old horses' hides
   In the hold of the Irish Rover.

4. We had sailed seven years when the measles broke
   out
   And our ship lost her way in a fog
   And the whole of the crew was reduced down to two
   'Twas myself and the captain's old dog.

Then the ship struck a rock, oh Lord, what a shock
And nearly tumbled over
Turned nine times around, then the poor dog was
    drowned
I'm the last of the Irish Rover

— o —

MOLLY MALONE
(Cockles and Mussels)

1. In Dublin's fair city
   Where the girls are so pretty
   I first set my eyes on sweet Molly Malone
   As she wheeled her wheelbarrow
   Through streets broad and narrow
   Crying, 'Cockles and mussels! Alive, alive-o!'
      Alive, alive-o!
      Alive, alive-o!
      Crying, 'Cockles and mussels!
      Alive, alive-o!'

2. She was a fishmonger
   But sure t'was no wonder
   For so were her father and mother before
   And they each wheeled their barrow
   Through streets broad and narrow
   Crying 'Cockles and mussels! Alive, alive-o!'
      Alive, alive-o!. . .

3. She died of a fever
   And no one could save her
   And that was the end of sweet Molly Malone.
   But her ghost wheels her barrow
   Through streets broad and narrow
   Crying 'Cockles and mussels! Alive, alive-o!'
      Alive, alive-o!. . .

Image of Christ – a page from the *Book of Kells*

Index